my tears turn into ink

faith foley

Legacy Book Press
LLC

Camanche, Iowa

ISBN: 979-8-9905387-0-2
Library of Congress Number: 1-14687206804

To my family, for supporting me and encouraging me in every way possible.

table of contents

lust over love

does the outside matter, when the inside is adequate?
are words more important than the touching of hands on a
summer evening?
to the teenage boy, it seems it is not.
hourglass figures, ticking time bombs, temporary lust, never
seeing love.
spurring slurs of lies just to get to see your shape.
they would rather see hips and waist than look you in your face.
the good ones never feel enough when they are all the
world needs.
the only difference is that we're not easy and are not a sleaze.
all we want is to give you love, hold you high, give you above
and beyond.
but you like the touch, the feeling.
you choose lust over love,
every
single
time.

-03/03/2020

charity

you use your words like you're giving to charity.
you spit them all out, although you never show you're there
for me.
you compliment me like the world is ending.
but you have enough time to break my heart again and again.
you look at me with those eyes like i am the first beauty
you've ever seen.
i don't feel special when you look like that at other people
besides me.
you think you're giving to charity
when you're just putting me into debt.
you think i don't see all the things you do when i'm looking
the other way.
i don't need you.
i don't need your fake charity.
but i still cash in your checks
at the bank on a rainy, melancholy day.

-03/03/2020

prove it.

she thinks it was a mistake that she chose you to be on her mind.
she knows it was a mistake to give her all to you when she
knew you would leave.
she knew that it was temporary; she still fought for your love.
prove her wrong.
prove to her that you'll stay.
prove to her that you'll be there for her every day.
listen to her cries and her chaotic life.
prove to her that you won't break her.

you see… she's already broken.
maybe not from your words or hands, but she's broken.
you used elmer's glue to try to fix her.
she was broken again, but with the remains of your lies
always stuck to her broken pieces.
one day, that girl will find someone with glue.
one day, she will have
support.
love.
a person to try and mend her demolished heart.

-03/03/2020

honey

sweet like honey,
you're stuck in my head.
you stick to my cloudy mind.
you may be sugary,
but too much of you is lethal.
dripping are your words of artificial sugar,
dropping into my ears,
covering my senses with lies.
you're made of wax,
so smooth and delicate,
but fake. unreal.
i could cure my sweet tooth with any other candy.
but i choose your artificial honey,
the delicious facade of being loved.
oh, how annoying the stick of your love is to my
unknowing heart.

-03/24/2020

eggshell

i pushed everyone away to be close to you.
i forgot about the laughs i had with others and invested all
my love into you.
now you are gone.
i sit alone every day, and i go to sleep alone every night.
i now realize how stupid it all was.
all the times we had together were fake.
fake laughs, plastic smiles, backstabbing lies.
now one year later, i sit alone.
i gaze at my eggshell white ceiling, with thick, hot tears
rolling down my face.
my chest rises heavily, my breath taken away.
i realize that nobody thinks of me, remembers me, or
wants me.
i fall asleep another night, waking up to another silent day.

-04/21/2020

silent

everything is always silent.
no other voices asking me about my day.
no other laughs, telling me my favorite joke.
no other cries, comforting me in my darkest moments.
i turned my ringer on silent.
i didn't check my notifications.
i ignored the people who cared,
to the extent that they forgot.
they stopped checking in.
they stopped caring.
and now i regret ever shutting them out.

-04/21/2020

fairytale

life is not a fairytale; problems are not being resolved on repeat.
the world is not candyland, with princes bowing down to
your feet.
it's not always sunshine, as clouds frequently cover up the sun.
there are no family tea parties, or friends having endless fun.
it all ends eventually, and all entities die sometime.
you don't always have people in your corner, and you don't
always have people on your side.
you don't have a magical fairy to make life great, but you
have beer and devil's dust to make you forget.
don't think about the rainbows; you can never reach the end.
and after you solve one problem, they will eventually start again.

-05/08/2020

temporary fullness

i went from nothing to everything.
i went from silence, to laughs, to cries, to not falling apart.
i went from being okay with loneliness to always craving more.
the minutes increase on how much i think of you.
it went from empty, to full of love, laughter, and happiness.
as i know it's temporary, i won't call this my new.
i will call it my short-term fullness.
of when i felt enough.
of when i felt needed.
of when i knew i was on someone's mind.

-05/24/2020

one more.

one crush onto another.
one heartbreak to the next.
rejection times five.
uncertainty times twenty.
but part-time happiness times one hundred.
sadly, that's one more set of beautiful eyes that don't look at
me the way i look at them.
one more smile, that is not smiling because of me.
one more boy, that will stay for a while, then leave to find another.
one more.
one more, until there is none left to be bothered.
just one more, until it's too much.

-05/24/2020

stability

i depend on you, but you always let me down.
i'm in a hole, not able to get out.
if i could make my living,
i would.
if i could survive on my own,
i would.
all i need is stability; is that too hard to grasp?
all i need is a figure to hold my hand; is that too much to ask?
i need stability.
stability to keep me warm; while i'm so young and tender.
i'm so fragile i could break in two.
stability is all i could ever crave, for my lonely, confused heart.

-06/08/2020

repeat

repeat the pain,
and then repeat the sorrow.
i loved him again like there was no tomorrow.
then tomorrow came, and i was broken.
the CD keeps spinning.
the part where i meet the boy.
the part where i fall for the boy.
the time when i was blinded by the boy.
the time when he never felt the same.
the realization that it was another lie.
the tape keeps playing.
repeat, repeat.
repeat the pain,
and then repeat the sorrow.
i loved him again like there was no tomorrow.

-06/20/2020

more than bronze

i get that i am not an average girl.
i don't have an average life, and i don't have anything
extravagant to show.

i don't waste my breath on being the center of attention.
i don't show off my body and my smile for friends.

but i have a heart… and damn, i will love with it.
but i have a brain… and i will make the right decisions for us.
but, i am not good enough.

i am not dripping in gold, and i do not cry any more than
bronze tears.

you don't want to explain to others i am way more than bronze.

you're not worth it, if i can't be showed off for the small
reason that i am concealed.
but, i am more than bronze. i am that gold medal, dangling
above you.

you're bronze, for listening to the crowd; not going for the
thing that makes you feel on top of the world.
for pushing away the one who truly cares and loves.
the one who nourishes your heart and listens on late nights to
your deep thoughts.

if you can't look past the fact that in public i appear bronze
but am truly gold, then i can accept i make excuses for you.

-06/26/2020

12

pink

i am stained pink.
from the residue of your lies
that hovers over the heart on my sleeve.

i am stained pink.
from the lingering noise,
of your laughter and kiss on my cheeks.

i don't want to be stained with your touch.
so bittersweet, i am swimming in a frozen lake.
50 below zero, you freeze my emotions into nothing.

you've pushed me away without even trying.
you're too horrible for me to love any longer.

-07/01/2020

defensive

i know the truth, but you try to lock it away with a key.
you know you're in the wrong.
but all you do is try and blame it on me.
you're the liar, the deceiver, being defensive to hide what's true.
just come out and tell me.
even if it makes me sad. even if it makes me blue.
you're so defensive.
i put you on the spot, and you don't realize that you've
already lost.
too angry for it to be unreal, you fell into your trap.
so now my heart, you will not steal.
i was wondering when i'd know from your words, but all i got
was ignorance sprouted into my ears.
you make yourself the victim, so you can keep playing
your games.
but little do you know... it's all the same.
i've heard the same lies planted in my field of memories.
they may have tricked me once, but you most definitely won't
get me twice.
you've always known i've hated liars.

-07/04/2020

six feet underground

six feet underground,
all i hear is the sound of your distant cries.
it is like the cries of help that poured out of my heart,
that you never heard.

six feet underground,
i feel nothing but dirt in between my toes.
i remember when i felt so much i wanted it all to stop.
you never noticed.

six feet underground,
i wish i was up there with you, but it had become too much.
no routine, but endless dreams.
no company, but endless uncertainties.
you never saved me.

-07/08/2020

gone.

gone again without a thought.
gone again without a warning.
they always leave right when my heart attaches to theirs.
they ripple out and are on their way.
i don't even have a say, or words to push out to make them stay.
it's happened too many times to be too torn.
but i still shed some tears, and it still raises my fears.
i should know not to get so attached.
i know they always leave.
but i still stay even after i am left all alone.
i sit, stuck in the thought that they will come back and love
me once again.

-07/15/2020

sitting by the fire

i am sitting by the fire,
letting the waves of heat rush on my face.
along comes the waves of realization,
that i'm all alone.
i am sitting by the fire,
letting the warmth dance on my skin.
my negative thoughts dance in my head.
i am sitting by the fire,
letting the wood burn and disintegrate into ashes.
my tears are cold, a rude awakening to the silence that
surrounds me.
i am sitting by the fire,
letting the crisp breeze tickle my cheeks.
i ponder why i am always misread.

-08/02/2020

misdirected

i am on my own,
but i can't be alone.
i am dreaming,
but i can't escape reality.
i need you,
but i know that you'll leave me torn.
i am misdirected and confused.
you leave me un-decisive and loveless.

-08/04/2020

my heart

my heart is too big, to dish out all my love.
i need the size, to support my lungs, and to reserve my smile.
i give away all my happiness, to make other people better.
i give away irreplaceable pieces of my soul, to help the mean,
soulless creatures i call home.
they leech on to me and i let them.
i let them suck the energy out of my heart.
my heart is damaged from when i began,
as it has been poked and bruised.
as it has been manipulated and tricked for entertainment.
my heart will forever pump blood slower,
love less,
cry more,
and trust none.

-08/19/2020

self-love

i need to find peace in the fact that love will find me. this isn't a game of 'i spy.' i need to stop searching for love, especially since i am in all the wrong places. it will lead to finding the wrong people, creating more stress and trauma. happiness will never be found if i don't help myself first. i have always been the type of person to put others before myself. i then question why i feel so inadequate.

i have recently realized the reason i am so drained and bruised is that i don't love myself. i don't take care of myself. i can't simply lie and say i don't have flaws. i can't lie about the fact that i hate myself more than anyone around me. if i'm so desperate to find love, even when it's toxic and wrong, why can't i be just as desperate to find love within myself? it's harmful to find love when you have none of it inside of your soul. it beats you down, taking all your worth from someone else's words and opinions.

i will not be searching for my other half, as if i found them now, it would be dreadful for us together. i need to love myself, before anyone else. that is the lesson everyone should be taught.

-08/21/2020

fog

the distance ahead of me is covered in thick fog.
dust covers up everything around me.
i can't find the exit from my clustered mind.
i am stuck amid memories.
i wait out the cloudy weather,
waiting for the sun to shine through my dark days.
the forecast predicts fog once again.
somedays it's rain, thunder, lightning.
i hide for shelter, from the world crashing around me.
all i want is a sunny day.

-08/29/2020

the book consisting of me.

i feel so close to you.
you have seen more than my cover.
you have peeked through almost every page.
you have flipped through my story,
and you still loved every piece.
even the stories on pages which were wilted, full of evil.
you still read them.
even the words in chapters that were covered in tears.
you helped dry them.
you have loved every single piece of me,
even when it's negative.
you have stuck by my side,
even when i was rude and ruthless.
you have read my book over and over,
and you understand the literature more and more each time.
you love me for me.
i don't have to pretend i'm something i'm not.
you accept me.

-09/05/2020

what kills me:

facing my reflection kills me.
i face all the flaws
and discover all my weaknesses.
a day full of silence kills me.
i feel unloved,
and realize i may be not on one soul's mind.
a moment of happiness kills me.
i know it won't last,
and two minutes later i'm left sulking in my loneliness.
a yell or slight loud noise kills me.
my head tells me i am unsafe,
and that i should react quickly.
many things kill me.
i can't handle the world around me.
i feel alone, left to conquer a life full of horrible demons.

-09/07/2020

admit it.

i see through you, so clear.
i feel what you feel, so strongly.
the signs are everywhere,
but you can't seem to read them.
you know what you need to say,
but you let your fear get in the way.
i'm right in front of you.
we could be together as two.
but you won't admit it.
you won't admit how you feel.
maybe it's confusing,
maybe your emotions are forever moving.
but i need you to say it.
i need you to admit it.
this cycle of jealousy and dishonesty is tiring.
admit it.
just please, admit it.
before it is too late to speak your words.

-09/12/2020

used

being used is like murder,
ripping apart the good in you until it is gone.
being used is torture, milking you dry of all the love you
possess in your soul.
you steal away my treasures and leave me with tainted glass.
i wonder how long this heartache you caused will last.
i want you so bad, so i give you what you want.
i give it all, even though i know deep down without it we
would most definitely drift.
i feel so drained for all that you ask of me.
i am so tiny, i can't give much more than i've already let go.
i want you to stay, but i know that my life can't keep working
out this way.
you are only nice when you need me.
you pretend to care when you only want to leave.
you act differently…
right when i give you what i ever so breathe.

-09/13/2020

encyclopedia

you treat me like i am an encyclopedia,
pushing out all my knowledge for your own needs.
you leave me on the shelf to gather dust,
to let my heart grow weeds.
when you need me, you pull me off the ledge.
you are giving me backhanded love and bleeding me dry.
believe me, i love you.
believe me, i try.
but i am not an encyclopedia.
you can't use me because you are too inattentive to follow
your own demands.
if you truly believe you can't do it, then why do you expect
me to have all the answers?
i am a human being.
i have a heart.
you know that, but you still treat me like i'm weight.
like i am the heaviness you must carry around in your backpack.
you use my love for you as a ticket to use me.
you flip through my pages and take away all my energy,
and my limited knowledge right along with it.
i am NOT an encyclopedia.

-09/13/2020

someone else

you hold onto me until you find someone better.
you use me, to give you love until someone more alluring
comes along.
you think i'm pretty until you see someone more beautiful
than i ever will be.
you think i'm smart until you catch someone who acts smarter.
you think i'm kind until someone with bad intentions shows
you affection.
you think i'll be yours, until you lose concentration and want
somebody who's temporary.
you think i'll stay, but i have almost had enough.
i give you one more chance,
but i will not let you once more choose lust over my love.
i'm genuine, and they are not.
i will give you what you need,
and they won't.
please stop searching for someone else,
when you already have me.

-09/13/2020

anger

anger is the result of mistreatment.
anger is the result of mistrust.
anger is the result of believing in you time and time again.
anger is the result of you letting me down,
breaking my already fragile heart in two.
anger is the result of you looking at me with seduction,
and then throwing it away the next day with ignorance.
anger is the result of loving you.
you're always on my mind,
and i am never on yours.

-09/14/2020

pictures

it makes me enraged that all i have is pictures.
fragments of memories sit in my lap,
and i wish they were alive.
i want current smiles.
i want present-tense love.
but all i have is a sheet of blurry film.
just a still second in my lifetime.
i need more than just a piece of paper.
i need you to be here.
but all i have is five-year-old events,
which i barely remember.
i try to grasp onto you,
but all i will ever have are photos.
i wish i were normal.
i wish that i could hug my mother after school.
i wish that i could tell her about my life problems.
that i could feel alive with her.
the only thing i have is a dead, lifeless, memory.
pieces of torn photographs, that only show a bit of my life
back then.
oh, how i wish i could remember you.
that i could have you now.

-09/15/2020

your remains

you left behind everything.
pieces of you are everywhere,
as we parted ways so quickly.
the clothes you used to wear still sit on some hangers in
the corner.
the perfume you used to spritz on yourself is still three-
quarters of the way full.
the vanity you used to sit at to do your makeup now stands in
my bedroom.
the picture frames you put together are still on the walls.
if your possessions are still here,
why aren't you?
why aren't your memories here?
why am i left here trying to remember who you were?
i search the web and gaze at all the photos.
i'll never be able to recreate who you were.

-09/16/2020

lemon tea

so sour, full of hatred from the past.
i don't know how much longer this anger will last.
the bitterness strikes my tongue,
and i spew frustration built up over the years.
i spill that acid-filled touch into your lemon tea,
along with my pungent fears.
swirl around that power of flavor into your drink,
and soak in the pain i have felt for eternity.
my sharp, sour, rage seeps through you.
my lemon antagonism pours into your tea.
i'm sorry i let my anger take over my words.
i'm sorry i let my traumatic lemon juice flow into your
uninterrupted sweet tea.

-09/17/2020

overthinking hours

this is the time when i think about thinking.
i think about the past.
about how i could've changed things to make everything last.
i think about the present.
about how i don't feel enough.
about how i could be better.
i think about the future.
about how i could have nothing.
that i could be minuscule and worthless.
i think too much.
i want it to all stop.

-09/17/2020

leave me.

i know you are going to leave me.
i can tell by the look in your eyes.
you are going to make me bleed.
i will bleed out the love inside of my heart.
i don't want you to leave,
because i know it will make me fall apart.
i can start to see the distance in your eyes.
you are beginning to question if you want me.
you are going to leave me all alone.
i'll again wonder what i did wrong.
why am i never enough?
why can't i be loved without any consequences?
they always leave me.
and i can't ever do anything to make them stay by my side.
so instead i lie to myself.
i tell everyone i didn't need them,
and that i'll be fine.
i'm not fine.

-09/17/2020

fireball

they are fumbling around from the whiskey.
whenever i see that booze bottle i can barely breathe.
they are tumbling down from the whiskey.
i can't make eye contact.
i get so nervous around anyone but me.
there are hands on me from the whiskey.
i am so vulnerable and young.
that's crystal clear to see.
there is foggy breath from the whiskey.
when you try to calm me down that cinnamon is all i inhale.
years of trauma from the whiskey.
it was only one night that will stay in my mind for eternity.
that fragile glass holds the whiskey.
you broke me just as easily.
that strong liquid forever is in my head.
a forever memory of the smell, and consequences received
from it.
intoxication will always be my biggest fear.
i have some hope that wouldn't have happened if fireball
whiskey wasn't there.

-09/18/2020

the welder and the metal

her wrists full of copper.
her head made of steel.
her stubbornness strikes you.
the metal is full of fear.
her bronze tongue screams at you.
you are directed to leave her alone.
but you still weld through the nickel.
you scrape the shininess away from her.
her metal is now dull,
and all her sparkle faded.
all because you took your tools,
and played your games that should never have been played.
now the metal is broken.
she is warped out of her once beautiful state.
she was used as a testing product,
and now is seen as waste.
she wishes you would have listened when she said to stay away.

-09/18/2020

reality of a woman

the world is full of creeps.
their eyes wander down me,
and my mouth tastes full of sour.
they can't keep their body to themselves,
and my lungs can barely breathe.
the world is full of danger,
as i can trust no man.
they might touch me with their strong and stealthy hands.
i isolate myself from the hurt,
because they might try to take my worth.
i am a woman,
and that shouldn't be an excuse.
but we are treated like toys,
like objects,
like we are created to be abused.

-09/18/2020

damaged or delicate?

sometimes i just want to move away.
i want to remove all my contacts and delete all social media.
i want to start over, letting go of the trauma and regrets of
the past.
i don't even want to say goodbye to all i've known.
i want to forget the pain i've received, and the toxic air i've
forever breathed.
i don't know what's keeping me here.
all this place does is remind me every day that i wasn't enough.
i wasn't enough for him. i wasn't enough for them. i'll never
be enough.
i want to start over somewhere.
where nobody knows me, leaving my dreadful memories
behind me.
maybe if i did that people would like me more.
i wouldn't be tarnished.
a damaged canvas full of runny, red paint.
i would be new, white, and polished.
i would be ready for the world to paint a colorful masterpiece
onto my heart.

-09/18/2020

incognito

the bad habit i have is to run away.
i overthink until it becomes a lie,
chasing around my heart and my mind.
i make up these scenarios that make my day a dread.
i think things and say things that should be left unthought
and unsaid.
i think it is best for me to leave.
my brain truly thinks they don't want or need me.
i turn off my powerful emotions,
along with my sweet words and genuine love.
i think they hate me when they don't,
i think it is best to leave them alone.
i turn off everything.
i become incognito.
i become reckless and passionless.
then i slowly slip away into the dark.
i think i'm better off alone.
here's a constant reminder for myself; you are not.

-09/18/2020

my excuses for you

irresistible, but irresponsible just is who you are.
i don't know if you are here for me, or if you are here to
create more scars.

you must've wanted fun, i figured.
to touch, to explore, and to vandalize.
you saw i wasn't an empty canvas, therefore you couldn't
place your art.
less like art, and more like ignorance in words and
incorrect feelings.

maybe you were lying, your words aren't true, and i should
let your actions shine through.
"it's just my personality."
so, then you're an inconsiderate flirt, and i throw your excuse
into the gutter.

maybe you knew what you were doing.
saw a broken girl, knew you had her heart.
for your own guilty pleasure, you thought it was fun to rip
it apart.

i make excuses for you because i don't want to know if the
problem is me.
i don't want to be broken, i want to be clean.

all i know is that your words are harsh.
so strong they struck my head.
i thought you were just a quiet boy, who didn't share his feelings.
turns out i was very misled.

-09/22/2020

shapeshifter

you shape-shift out of love with me when i don't have
something you need.
you turn a cold shoulder and leave my heart to bleed.
you go from being lovely to despising me.
even though i never do anything to cause you to leave.
you form into a monster.
you lie through your teeth.
you know it hurts,
and you know it devastates me.
then you shape into everything i need.
you love me so desperately.
you're a shapeshifter and you love to torment me.
you walk all over me as you please.
i know deep down inside you most likely love me.

-09/24/2020

culture

it is culture for you to skin the flesh from my bones.
for you to tear away the innocence from my precious existence.
it is your custom to break my heart in two.
each section of the organ pulsing in pain.
you fill me with sorrow.
i am overfilling until i am running on empty.
you show me the tradition of developing my trauma.
it is your favorite part to scar my eyes and brain.
it is your culture to ruin me and kill me slowly with your words.

-09/28/2020

the devil

the devil was once an angel.
you were once kind,
having the best intentions in mind.
you warped into something unknown,
the sound of your screams echoing in my head.
you were once innocent,
your passion dancing on my skin.
you are now fiery with horns,
piercing my heart and letting it bleed.
you were once my friend.
your words so delicate,
holding my soul.
you are now spitting flames,
burning my chest into embers and ashes.
i shouldn't have trusted you,
as i can trust no one.
even an angel can become the devil.
even someone so lovely can become miserably evil.

-10/07/2020

starving

the sight of it makes you sick,
but you can't escape it.
the mirror is your worst enemy,
even though the reflection shining through is pure beauty.
excuses, excuses,
you use them to look like everyone else.
you say you don't need it,
but you do.
otherwise, you are run down and feeling blue.
add in a substitute to trick your mind,
but know that what you're doing is dangerous.
you are playing with fire.
you are slowly warming until you are in flames far from return.
you are going down a bad path,
only because your eyes are deceiving you.

-10/09/2020

oranges

shove them down your throat.
you feel the tingle and tell yourself it is progress.
juice them,
the pulse and remains squish into your body.
you force them back out,
and you know that it is wrong.
you feel guilt every time you make orange juice.
but you are so addicted to the taste.
it burns your heart.
and loosens your sleeves.
you think this is the only way to go,
but all it does is make your knees weak.
your bones fragile.
and your heart feels defeated.
it will never be enough,
and you will never stop.
until everything you had is long lost.

-10/09/2020

do you even feel remorse?

slipping through your fingers,
the feeling of gratitude escapes,
sinking into the unknown.

crack.

you feel your heart pulsing,
little drips of blood
falling onto nothing.

crunch.

you are slowly breaking,
all remorse flooding into your soul,
when you remember who you truly are.

tear.

you relive the moments when you were full of horror and harm,
and feel guilt for all that you have accomplished.

break.

how does it feel to be seen as great in the eyes of the devil?
how does it feel to be so sick, ruining the minds of others for
your own enjoyment?

devastation.

you rip away everything.
you scar their minds,

and blow smoke into their lungs.
they burn for eternity from your fiery touch.

-10/12/2020

you must keep going.

you swipe away the hair that falls in your eyes.
you walk down the long road, while it slips over your face.
you wipe away the locks of gold that sprout down your head
onto your shoulders.
you continue down the path,
and it falls again and again.
it is blinding your vision and covering your snowy complexion.
it's dark and cold,
and you keep traveling to your destination.
even when you can't see,
you slow and move the strands covering your bright eyes.
you go on steadily,
and you work your way through the storm.

-10/12/2020

running away from death

i am running away from death,
but it follows me consistently.
i am nearly empty,
chasing after satisfaction to fill me.
i am no longer feeling alive,
begging the lord to fill me with life.
the dread of the day is always hiding in my sleeves.
the waves of darkness steadily hover over me.
i wish for light to shine through the shades,
but i am afraid it may always stay dark,
and i will always feel astray.

-10/12/2020

shades of green

i can see the jealousy,
a deep shade of green.
you pounce on the accusations,
and you never believe me.
the insecurity is an emerald,
hidden in the rock that is your heart.
it is peeking through;
only the observant can see the real you.
i can read you like literature,
flipping through the statements,
and learning how to love you.
i can see the sadness,
a murky flaw that is masked with burning red anger.
your hazel eyes pierce through me,
and the jealousy is revealed,
along with your pain and fears.
you are only shades of green.
monochromatic, and i can see everything.

-10/13/2020

bee sting

the poison injects into my body.
the toxic sensation flows through my veins.
you are a bee that keeps stabbing my heart time and time again.
it burns, and it leaves bruises,
but the honey trail you leave tastes too sweet.
i can't let go of you,
even though you fill me with poison with your painful sting
every day.
you swarm my head and attack my feelings daily.
oh, how my sweet fragrance attracts so many deadly dangers.

-10/14/2020

quiet

there are so many reasons you possess me day to day.
not prone to being vulnerable—you make it possible to
protect myself from evil.
not saying the wrong thing—you make me say nothing at all,
and no anger erupts.
no entity knows my plans—you make it so nobody knows
my next move, and that i can be safe in my actions through
and through.
you help shelter me from humankind.
even if it means i may lose a few opportunities.
i have quiet infested in me like a wasp nest.
and if you come close, they will sting you away.
it's only fair i be alone, so i don't have any sick prices to pay.

-10/15/2020

you are red.

your red lies, red anger, red clothes.
you cover me in blood.
blood that drips down the edges of my heart.
you take your red, resentful eyes and rip me apart.
you are a demon feasting off my pain,
your red hands gripping my fragile soul.
i want you to let go of me,
but it seems you haven't lost control.
your red anger burns my lungs,
and i am taken captive by your devious grin.
i can't breathe anything but the smoke you ooze out of your
red body.
and i cannot speak words to save myself from this never-
ending torture.
sentences of despair have not escaped from my mouth.
i will stay quiet, held down in your devastating red passion.
it is a draining cycle, but i will take it.
it is not what i deserve, but i can't leave you behind.

-10/20/2020

forever means nothing.

i am highly strung,
because there are strings attached.
i am concerned with my future,
because i know we'd never last.
i want forever with you,
but all i have is doubt—
and a need to escape.
the aroma filled with rosebuds fills the room,
along with the silence.
it was made from losing the battle we fight together every day.
words are exchanged,
and anger rises within us.
it has become too much,
and we have shut down completely.
forever seems to mean nothing.
our hearts are distant from one another.
it has ended, and all that is needed is for us to move on with
our bodies and souls.

-10/24/2020

give me a pinky promise.

tell me you love me and make it a promise.
wrap your pinky delicately around mine, and make your
words last forever.
hold my hand throughout the night and kiss my cheeks with
much delight.
your touch is so soft, you tell me everything i would ever
want to hear.

your pinky slowly un-tightens, and you take back phrases
slowly, day by day.
you start to mean what you say less and less.
and you seem more distant, as our eyes don't meet near as often.

your pinky is ripped away from mine, and harsh words are
screamed in my face.
you broke the promise that we would last forever.
you tell me you never meant it and my pinky is left raw from
the absence of your love.

pinky promises are a thing to never be used.
as they will run away, leaving you broken and bruised.
nobody intertwines their pinkies, and nobody promises their
love, because it gets your heartstrings tugged and tugged.
tugged until nothing is left except for loneliness,
and the regret you ever gave your pinky to any other soul.

-10/26/2020

stuttering is my profession

i forever stutter as i can't grasp what to say.
i jumble my words, and i get frustrated that i sound this way.
i hate being shy, and i cannot do what needs done.
i am never able to tell someone no,
and i forever fight in silence to be more authoritative.
i do whatever someone commands, like a trained dog on a leash.
pull my chain and i will follow, as my vocabulary doesn't
include any phrase to say n-o.
i constantly trip over every word that escapes from my
mouth, when i rarely try to explain my fears and doubts.
whenever i am heard i am hushed.
and then people put up a huff when i don't preach everything
i have to say.
i will forever listen when given an assignment,
and i will never defy anyone even if it's what i so ever crave.
stuttering and stuttering is all i will ever do.
trip-ing over my—words. will nev-er stop.

-10/26/2020

the apparatus

the ghost of you possesses my soul when i least expect it. you
hover over me, draining my energy.
i feel defeated, and you suck the life out of me.
i try to speak my words, to get you to understand.
you do nothing but hurt me, even when i lend you a
helping hand.
i have had enough of your apparatus, and i now need to face
the truth.
i must leave you behind, even though in the past i couldn't
get enough of you.
i'm sorry you treat me like a boy treats his action figures.
i'm sorry that you speak words that freeze my heart until it
crumbles in insanity.
i'm sorry that you don't deserve one piece of my soul, though
you still pull it out of me.
i'm sorry that i'm apologizing for all that you have done.
it is because i feel sorrow for leaving you alone.

give me chills with your eyes, you pierce right through me,
and i feel that i am running out of time. i need to get away, i
need to escape. you break and bruise me, with no remorse.

-11/03/2020

you put me through withdrawal

i am addicted to you.
i am addicted to toxic love, and when my heartstrings are tugged.
i am addicted to the thought of losing you, a never-ending
battle in my mind.
i am addicted to the regrets, of when i said things i should've
kept a secret.

i feel withdrawn when you leave me, as your dangerous
dosage is needed to keep me on my feet.

though you are a rushing current sweeping me under into
the depths of the deep blue sea.

though you are a flame that catches my house on fire,
burning the memories and creating a disastrous heat in
my heart.

though you are the frostbite on a winter night, fifty below
zero and freezing my soul until my teeth clatter and my
lungs crack.

you put me through withdrawals, and my head hurts at the
thought of you.
you make me hallucinate.

you make me play a jazz song, singing along with the blues.

you make me scream my soul out of my chest, tears rushing
down my cheeks.
a cold reminder that you are not here.

you make me wish we never met, regretting that i ever
loved you.

-11/03/2020

the beauty the world holds in her hands

grass blades,
sharp enough to give you some discomfort.
a fresh aroma gives you gratitude that you can see the sun.
flowers so pretty, but a bee could be waiting to sting if you
linger too close.
so many colors for all but the down to see.
as the sulking people only see black, white, and grey.
a melancholy look, forever forced on their face.
the sun shines down on the heads of the known,
and the forgotten hide in the rain clouds waiting until dusk.
forever alone, they never know that life is full.
full of love.
all they see is the earth that is filled with hunger.
a craving for power, a destiny never to be achieved.
we don't see the sun.
we don't see the flowers on a spring morning,
and we don't feel the wind brushing our cheeks.
we see blue.
we see dark.

-11/11/2020

this one is different?

i wish i could tell you about this one boy.
about the way he makes my heart flutter,
and how he makes me forget all my fears.
or about how his delicate thumb wipes away my warm tears.
all i want is to show you his sweet smile,
and his innocent eyes as he makes me melt inside.
i want you to see, how much this one means to me.
i want you to see that i have found someone who provides
me joy,
as you would be proud to see i am happy.
i wish.
i wish you were here to see,
how much this one means to me.

-11/15/2020

my world is yours

i held the world out in my hands,
ready to give you every square inch of the earth.
i offered everything,
ready to give up my heart and soul,
only to be yours.

but you wouldn't walk your two feet a step onto my land.

-11/16/2020

the silent sentience

i am broken beyond repair.
full of misery,
the terrors of trauma forever prey on my heart.
i am hell,
the devil with horns,
trashing the lives of others.
i am so negative,
the smiles that come upon others are ripped away by my frown.
i need to stay away from the joyful,
as i fill them with doubt.
i am a perfect pair with evil,
as they are my cooperatives in this game of sulking days.
i only deserve the bad,
as i have harmed the lives of many good.
sadness is the way to how i live,
as happiness is locked away with a key never to be found.
i live in fire,
the flames and dust arise within my soul.
i am bad.
and i suck the life out of everything i've ever loved.

-11/30/2020

self-sabotage
(a constant battle between myself and i)

will i be fine on my own, or will i regret what i've lost?
will i go my way by myself; or will i pay the cost?

my mind keeps telling me that i need to be alone.
but i don't know if it's just messing with me, because self-sabotage is all i know.
bad habits. my head tells me i don't need them.
my mind plays games, a constant battle.
a debate, yelling into microphones arguing that this is good for me.
but my opponent, the messed-up mastermind inside these walls, convinces me otherwise.
my head is world war three, a fight for freedom from the words spilt in my brain. tearing me down by the tears in my eyes, and the fear in my heart.
my heart knows all that i deserve, but my powerful mind overpowers and takes me to all i've ever known.
again. again. again.
pain is all i remember, so when happiness comes along i run the other way.
back to what i'm used to.

-11/30/2020

ticking time bomb

you will never believe that i breathe for you.
you will never believe that all my time is dedicated to seeing
you smile.
i am seen as a deceiver, because my head tells me what's
better, then my heart tells me to go forward.
i am seen as a liar, because i backed out on my words, my
fear coming over me.

i am sorry if you can never love me again.
i am sorry if my words slip through your heart like glass cuts
through skin.
i am sorry if your soul was swept away by the wind when i
said what's haunting me in my mind.
i am sorry that i am not ready to give you all of me.

i am not ready. i am not ready to show my love with needles
of responsibility poking in my sides.
i am not ready to show you everything; being vulnerable is a
scary occurrence.

wait for me, as i will come back, my heart open for your
beautiful, genuine soul.

-12/1/2020

the absence of you

hold me in your arms,
and sing me a gentle lullaby.
soothe me with your hugs,
and wrap my soul in your warmth.

that is the way it was supposed to be.

all i get is the absence of your scent.
and the empty feeling that you are not here.
days go on and you slowly slip further back into my mind.

goodbye is the only thing i hear from your voice.

you are gone,
and i am left confused in this melancholy world.

-12/2/2020

when you were gone

you drained the pacific out of my ocean eyes,
when you slipped away into the shadows.
you stole the consistent pump that works my heart,
when you said i was nothing, and that i was never enough.

my life is a daze,
fazing in and out of reality.
my life is walking to an unfulfilled destination, with an
unforgettable journey.
a never-ending ache in my chest and pounding in my head.

useless breathes of when i am pushing through the days,
i wonder what would be different if nothing had changed.
but nothing is the same.
you're gone,
and my soul went with you when you left.

-12/22/2020

what do you think love is?

what do you think love means?
is it the way you feel when they look at you?
or is it deeper than that?
is it the way they kiss you in the morning, the sun shining
through shutters?
or is it more than that?

is love a thing that is easy to grasp?
or do you work a minuscule wage barely finding what you need?
is love a job?
hard work needed with dangerous accessories?

what is love?
is it something that has already been discovered?
is it still unfounded?

-12/27/2020

i didn't even get a funeral.

i didn't even get a funeral for you.
watching you crumble out of my hands with no memoir.
you thought that no explanation was needed when you
slipped into your casket.
you didn't plan the dates for after your last day,
and you failed to inform the ones you know that we would be
left to pick up your pieces.
years of offices, thousands of bills.
they were always taking notes.
they were always watching.
because of you.
i didn't get to see you in your casket.
i didn't get to grieve what i had lost.
i didn't get to see you get lowered into the ground.
and i didn't get to toss a black petunia, a goodbye from me
to you.
you were just gone,
and i hate you for that.

-01/16/2021

too much time; p a s s e s

we have conversations with our mouths closed.
no sound is spoken as we can hear each other clearly.

we meet our eyes together almost as often as our lips.
that piercing gaze makes the hours go by

a little too hastily,
a little too much.

the time ticks…
and all distractions are discarded.

i feel bad for forgetting.
every other person disappears.
and they get angry with me.

they feel a little too dissatisfied.
they feel as if they are non-important.

i am sorry to the ones i have ignored.

i am just a girl dealing with a case of
puppy love.

those eyes suck me in,
and those are the only things i gaze at until the sun rises the
next morning.

i check my phone, and i see how time has passed without
a thought.

i miss them the second they leave.
even though i know,
they will be here,

the very next day.

-01/20/2021

5/10/17 (when innocence was stolen)

she lost the last crumbs of herself.
may tenth.

she felt like she was now forever missing.
may tenth.

tears rolled onto the borrowed pillow; regret latched onto her
head; she chose to come here.

she thinks may tenth could have been a skipped day.
she thinks that may tenth could have been avoided.

it was just supposed to be a sleepover.
laughs and giggles, then crashing asleep with your friends.

an uninvited guest came to visit,
may tenth.

the guest went on to hurt her,
and stole her.
she's now gone, never to be returned.

-01/21/2021

the plant and his overgrown roots

they say to cover up a seed with plenty of dirt, to let it sprout.
they say to plant it in a pot, covering the roots so it doesn't
become distraught.

what would happen if the roots peeked out of the soil?
would the plant rot,
or would people see the plant differently?
would the plant be unhappy,
that all his roots are in the open, for everyone to see?

would the plant and the people learn to accept the crazy
weeds and roots that grow out uncontrollably?
would it become the new normal, to show every piece of the
plant out in the open, for everyone to judge?

-01/31/2021

i'm your wonderland

you said i'm your wonderland.
that i occupy your mind every second of every day.
i see your eyes are filled with love, when you look at me.
i see the smile creeping on your face, when i walk in the room.

i like being someone's wonderland.
i enjoy having someone think of me just as much as i think
of them.

-02/04/2021

dancing in her storm

he decided to dance in her storm.
he realized that her storm was acid rain.
a hurricane that swept him off his feet.
the toxic waste carried him away,
into the eye of the hurricane.

her gaze lured him in,
out of the sun.
and she sucked him into the depths of her deeper water.

he struggled to swim,
as her storm was pure poison,
nothing you would expect from a girl like her.

she was a delicate summer day,
an innocent breeze with the sun shining out of her.
she was everything he **thought** he wanted,
and everything he would ever need.

little did he know that the weatherman predicted a hurricane
just a little bit later in the day.

-02/18/2021

the point of view of: JRM

i never knew that it would end up this way.
alone—never knowing what and where.
i try to blame my past for everything i've said and done.
people are starting to see through it.
i don't like that people see my true color through the facade.

i used and used and abused.
it took me apart—i've lost everything i've ever known. i
should've gotten help. but i kept going—killing myself more
and more.
i hurt the hearts of others. i miss them every day.

i wonder what has changed since i have been gone. do
they miss me—like i wish to see them every waking hour?
i haven't been there to see them grow up. i now never have
seen them go through the stages of early life—the most
important times of their sentience. and i may never see
them again.

do they hate me? do they even remember my existence? i'm
so sorry that i hurt you. i feel like opiates are the only option.
i need them to mask all the pain i feel. the pain of losing my
sister. the pain of losing my father. all the pain from years of
being manipulated by men.

i know that isn't an excuse. i know that i am so utterly selfish,
leaving you all behind for my own absorbed reasons.
i wish i could hold you in my arms. i remember the last time
i saw you. you said goodbye so suddenly — i knew i would
never see you again.

i walked out — to pursue my hobby of dust and spoons. i left you guys because i was too weak to fight. believe me, i regret all that has occurred. i wish i could take it all back — but destiny tore us apart.

i know you are angry with me — and that burning flame may never die down into embers. but just know that i love you. i may not come back from this. i may not be strong enough to fight the devil's call. he is pulling me deeper and deeper into nothing. my head is getting darker and darker every time that needle sticks into my forearm.

i remember the day i said those sharp words. they sliced through her heart, cutting right through it. i hurt her — her happiness never to be returned. it was almost like torture, the evening i screamed "i hate you" in her young face.

i remember the times i left them all alone. they were dependent, but i still left them. i would leave it up to them to protect each other. schizophrenia and pedophilia were allowed in my home — to take advantage of my daughters. i never seemed to notice.

i knew they were depressed. i could see the dark circles and desperation in their eyes. i never took any action. i let them sink deeper into their heads. she will now never be able to properly communicate with others. she was so alone, she never got to talk with other kids. for the rest of her life, she will be unable to stand in a crowd, without feeling defeat.

i would lock them out. hours i would sit on my bathroom floor, letting the adrenaline rush through my veins. they would beg and knock for me to come out. it always took ages for me to finally open the door. my arms would sprinkle onto the ceiling, a mixture of heroin and my blood splattered onto the walls. the stain still sticks.

like the stain, my memory sticks in their heads. a complex mess that can't be wiped away with a damp cloth. they scrub and scrub with hundreds of dollars, the therapists tell them what they need to hear. they try to rip away every image of me in their head, but i have oozed into every single crevasse and crack.

i will forever leave residue in their hearts and heads. it clogs up their mind and soul, and they slowly must gather control of all that i have stolen. i am a thief, as i have taken everything they called theirs. they will be left gathering it years and years ahead, as i am still grasping onto it all.

i have broken into their home and cracked their foundation. the house that sits above is rocky, and the house rumbles every time a voice is raised in their direction. i have ruined the crucial parts of construction, and the house will never be sound. the stained-glass windows are dim and have small cracks around the edges. i crushed the panes and they are left too broken to repair it.

-02/26/2021

the cycle of possession - happening in me

the negative energy inside of people possessed me.
i was drawn towards the people hiding in the dark,
with the evil souls, and bad intentions.
at the time, i thought they were a friend, someone i could
lean on.
i had learned after time, that they were just sucking the
happiness out of my heart.

but then there was one person,
who broke the chain.
the cycle of me falling, and being used, abused.
their pure heart of gold overpowered the people conjuring me.
they took me out of the dark,
and showed me the light.

now i bask in the sun every day.
while they hold my hand.
keeping me safe,
i am forever away from the people who had tricked me in
the past.

-03/07/2021

before time was still

the vase sits on the dusty windowsill,
a remembrance of the last time a rose was sitting in the sunshine.
the dishes had piled up in the sink over time;
though once the sink was empty, a shine glazed over the facet.
one time the shades were opened,
without a layer of dust shadowing the sun.
there used to be voices bouncing in the walls of this house.
laughter, and "i love you" used to dance in the halls while a
record spun in the corner.
it pushed out the waves of a beautiful melody.

now the dust and silence take over every inch of where
happiness used to roam.
everything is still.

-03/16/2021

i never knew what love was,
but now i am an expert.

i wish somebody would have told me **what it felt like** to fall in love.
i wish i would've had the knowledge to know it was coming so soon.
i would have wanted to know that an individual could become so important to me, in the blink of an eye.
i think it is miraculous that i **found someone who didn't want to hurt me.**
i found someone that **holds me** when i need them.
a person who **gives me everything,**
even when i don't want it.
as i fall deeper into love,
i'm thankful nobody told me.
love is full of beautiful surprises.

-03/17/2021

i give second chances

a second chance is a risk,
most are willing to take.
it is a thing that many people abuse,
an addiction to take in the rejected repeatedly.

most people don't deserve second chances,
but they are handed out for free on rainy, sunny, and
snowy days.
they cloud your judgement with the "i'm sorry" and they
hurt you again,
even if you think they have changed.

-03/17/2021

will you leave?

every time your feet pass through the doorway,
i watch your figure walk into the distance.
i wonder if you will ever come back.
a voice in my head tells me you will be gone forever.
maybe it is because of the many times people have stopped
coming back.
they had said goodbye,
and then never returned into my life.
i have deep thoughts about all the people i have lost.
how i will never see them again.
i do not want you to leave also.
because you are so much more to me,
than any of them.

-03/24/2021

promises made to me.

in my lifetime,
there have been countless broken promises.
"i'll be back."
one i heard multiple times from my own mother.
"i miss you!"
dozens of time that slipped out of my best friends mouth.
later i find out she wanted to ruin me, and all that i thought i
was worth.
"i won't do it again."
i heard from their mouths in all the same tones.
it repeats in my head as i think about how they struck me
with pain and heartache once more.
"i am not lying!"
one i've heard the most.
i had evidence,
that your tongue was spitting out everything but the truth.
there are these broken promises, that run through my mind
every time a pinky is pointed in my direction.
every time i hear promises i remember the past,
and i cannot think of one time a promise was kept.

-04/06/2021

love is real.

sunset kisses,
passionate wishes,
you brought me more love than a soul could ever crave.
you fulfill my dreams, as you caress my cheeks,
you are all i would ever need.
you call my name after what feels like decades of being alone.
you show me what it feels like to be alive.
thank you for the everlasting,
soul-grabbing,
romance you have shown me.

-04/26/2021

i'm not just seldomly sad...

i sweetly sob,
as tomorrow begins.
a strike of tears,
a roll of the dice,
i feel more alone now than i ever have.
i didn't even think twice,
to assume life was easy now.
i have more to live for,
but i now think of more ways to die.
the tears drop like rain on windows when it's a cloudy day.
my heart sinks in my chest,
like an anchor sinking its teeth into the ocean floor.
i feel like puking,
the worst stomach bug you could ever catch.
but the sickness is all in my thoughts.
my pillow holds my head,
and my sheets hold my hands.
for i will never return to the day i am free.

-05/10/2021

the first scare

the first scare,
that let my heart sink deep into my chest.
she was hiding,
beating quietly because she was terrified.
there again the first scare,
that made my lungs slow down.
she was quiet so nobody found her.
i never knew what fear felt like.
anxiety and nervousness always lived in these walls,
but the real heart racing,
mind and thoughts pacing,
suffocating fear found me this morning.
my life was almost over,
until it was fake,
and normalcy begun once again.

-06/22/2021

i'm different

i've been held close to everyone's standards since i was a
little girl.
a little pretty, a little organized.
good grades, good standards.
that girl i once was, never was happy.
that girl held her crumbling heart close in her chest,
as people told her all the things she needed to be in their image.

change is a thing one cannot avoid, or plan.
change means growth,
which is necessary when living life.
people never enjoy the thought of difference.
they never see the good in when things are no longer the same.

i was a very sad person.
i constantly thought about people's approval,
and who they thought i was.
i'd pay attention to the things that didn't matter,
and would work to save myself from judgment.
that girl was exhausted, never being able to breathe.
depression was a dark cloud over my head.

as any person would,
i changed.
people left,
people came,
and i grew older.
a normal thing that happens to every sentient,
made people i love break me down.

i didn't commit a crime,
i didn't commit a felony.

all i did was fall in love.
i found someone that washed away the pain, and kept the girl
who was once lonely from falling into the dark.

the happiness i feel,
is a disappointment to everyone.
i broke the standards everyone held me in for fifteen years,
and now it feels they don't need me anymore.

i am not something to be proud of anymore.
i didn't get an A+.
i didn't keep all the friends that treated me like shit.
i didn't answer a phone call,
because i was enjoying my life off a screen.

i am "slipping."
i am "slacking."
i am "an entirely different person."

i have just grown,
out of the girl who always cried,
and never felt enough.

-07/09/2021

how, when, or why.

tops that **don't fit,**
knots that **won't untie,**
things have changed, never to be the same.
the scale tells me a higher number every time my body
hovers on it.
over time you ignore it,
the hundreds of dollars you wasted on the new clothes.
they **are too tight already,** a month after getting them.
you forget the feeling of fabric letting your chest breathe.
a feeling of relaxation,
knowing **no one can see the outline of your body.**
that is no longer a thing you experience.
you ignore the people always whispering that you are
different.
and that they no longer know who you are.
i didn't decide to change,
change is just a thing that happens as a mortal ages.
**a body isn't the only thing that morphs into
something you don't recognize.**

-07/09/2021

89

my sunshine

your skin is soft,
and your smile is sweet.
you always have a shine in your eyes,
and you always comfort me.
i love you in so many ways,
and i love the way you're gentle with me.
how you calm me when i am afraid.
there's nothing i could say, write, or do to show you the way
you make me feel.
my heart was once sinking, but now it is floating.
you make it flutter, and there's an ache in my chest from the
love i hold for you.
i love everything about my boy,
my sweet sunshine.
i love everything about you,
because you are my favorite thing.

-07/21/2021

i need a friend.

secrets, shared with my mind; because i have no one to tell
them to.
a sad, hard life; and i'm dealing with it all alone.
when you say that you have my side…all of it is a fucking lie.
if you meant that promise you'd be here tonight.

i need a friend, someone to tell my secrets to.
i need a person that i can breathe with, someone that i can
be me with.
and i know that it's hard to see, but i need someone here
with me.
because i need a friend.

i need you, even though you aren't here for me.
i love you, even though you want to kill me.
if it means anything to you, i'd do anything for you.
i wanted to tell you, what i think you think of me.
i bet you wish i were someone else, somebody better, than
what i am now.
and i'll treat you better. because you're everything that i need.

-10/01/2021

unhappy-

unhappy-
a word that describes me quite often.
an adjective that slips off the tongue when you think about
how the world wraps around devastation.

the way people are brought up and taught changes the
universe. it changes the state of mind of any person,
they are forever affected by the words of mankind.

depression-
a common occurrence in any human, a sinking, dark cloud
that blinds you eternally. the dark eyes and empty smiles
make up the population of planet earth.

you would like to think there is one person with no
experience of sin.
you would like to think there is one person who hasn't
danced and followed the devil's rules.
you think that there is one person. you discover there is not.
you know that every person is bad.
you bleed internally, until it seeps out of your heart, your
eyes, and your mouth. and then you die; unhappy.

-10/07/2021

clueless

a person so clueless of the devastation around them likely
caused the destruction.

you must suffer in silence; you cannot cause disruptions.
there is nobody to help you when you act like this is normal.
you can't escape if everyone only sees perfection.
internally you are aware; that life is on the downhill.
you cry until you fall on your knees. you cannot take this pain
any longer.

everyone is clueless. even yourself.
you put on the perfect show,
and now everything seems perfect.

you are dying; your heart is bleeding out quicker every day.
a clueless little girl.

-10/07/2021

white picket fence

i've made too many decisions; i'm just a little kid playing adult.
it's too late to go back to the old days.
i'm forced to grow older.
my days consist of worrying.
is my life going to be like my biggest fear?
am i going to feel this way forever?
will the world change around me, or am i just waiting to die?
i want the white picket fence.
i want the happy life.
i'm so scared that i'm never going to get that.
i don't want to be disrespected.
i don't want to be miserable until the day i finally die.
i'm so scared.
is my life going to be this way forever?

-10/07/2021

dancing on the sun ~~(sinking into the moon)~~

so happy,
so smiley,
i love my life more than anything!
~~please help me.~~
the way i thought life should be is how my life is going!
~~i want to give up; save me.~~
i'm looking at and striving toward my future,
i cannot wait to grow up!
~~i don't want it to be this way…i want to die.~~
~~the one above is a criminal, taking every happy thing away~~
~~from me.~~
~~i don't want to stay, even for the people i truly love.~~
i love all my responsibility, it makes me stronger and more
capable for the future!
~~someone please take the boulders off my shoulders, i am~~
~~slowly losing my breath and my arms are growing weaker.~~
i am finally happy, after years of torture.
~~every smile is a lie, i feel worse than i ever have before.~~

-12/22/2021

95

matches aren't reusable darling

silky sheets and lots of sleep don't help what's in my head.
a nutritional breakfast, and a check off on my bucket list
doesn't make me forget what has happened to me.
hunger pains and punches remain in the back of my mind,
even though my stomach is full, and my skin is clear of bruises.
my life is a cardboard match, not a lighter.
i'm burnt and charred beyond use.
there are no refills, reuses, or second chances.
i am damaged, deranged, and unusable.
it is time for the embers sizzling on the match to be chilled
with liquid water.
you will hear it fizzle out like the sound of a whisper, telling
you to keep the secrets you already know.

-01/24/2022

do you ever have the urge?

do you ever have the urge to slit your wrist, and watch the blood drip down onto your knees?

do you ever have the urge to dunk your head underwater, until you can no longer breathe and your heart stops beating?

do you ever have the urge to eat your favorite bottle of "candy" in your medicine cabinet until your mouth foams and your skin peels?

do you ever have the urge to set yourself on fire with the matches in your kitchen cupboard?

do you ever have the urge to find the tallest building and sky dive from it, and then "forget" your parachute?

do you ever have the urge to end it all with no second thought because nothing in this world is more craved than death?

me too.

-02/02/2022

lucifer will teach you a lesson
for damaging my soul.

i was 11, the day you took my soul.
i was 11 the day i was violated into despair,
leaving me broken for eternity.
i was a little girl, i had only been on earth a small amount
of time.
YOU were a grown being, with experiences and lessons.
YOU were an adult, and i was a baby.
you hurt me.
you… broke me.
you. you make me cry soft tears every time i think of being
touched in an intimate manner.
you, ruined a little girl forever. just to satisfy your
disgusting needs.
i am so torn apart,
i cry when i am touched the wrong way.
i cry whenever i see something that reminds me of the
monster you are.
i shake in fear every time i see a truck that resembles yours.
i will never have a normal romantic relationship, due to your
irresponsibility and fucked up state of mind.
your sick enjoyment of ripping away a kid's innocence makes
me shiver in anger and fear.
you deserve to go to hell and burn in the hottest flames
down there.
i hope the devil himself lights you into flames while you
scream in misery.
"i'm sorry! i'm sorry!" you will scream as you cry in pain.
but lucifer will laugh at you, as even though he is the devil,
the man is not as deranged and fucked up as you.
you're a nasty pedophile.

-02/06/2022

neglecting mind, body, and soul

i looked into the mirror today.
my eye-bags seemed to overtake my blue irises.
i noticed my mouth earlier this morning.
it feels dry, parched of water. my lips are peeling and pale.
i noticed my bed late last night, it was caving in as i couldn't
get out of it that day.
i don't feel so good.

maybe a nap will help, and i can rest my eyes.
maybe some water will quench my thirst.
maybe some chapstick will heal the bloody cracks on my lips.
maybe if i eat a salad, i will stop having my stomach turn
and bloat.

i cannot heal my deteriorated body with some "self-care."

maybe, therapy is all i need.
        pills
        help

-10/19/2022

processing life without you is hard:

it is hard to process the fact that i don't have a mom, when i am supposed to.

it is even harder to process the reality that she had a choice to stay, but still walked out of the door.

knowing that she is living and breathing every day without me there is painful.

it is difficult to realize that my day to day is normal for me, even though there is an important structure missing.

i should not have to be used to a life like this, but i am…after 7 out of 17 years alive living without a maternal parent.

the memories continue to fade as i grow older, and i wonder if i ever cross her mind.

-11/16/2022

red velvet kiss

she rocks her **red velvet** lip-gloss, ignoring her torn lips, and her broken heart.
have you known her strength?
she may be meek and small, but her mind has endured a lifetime of disaster.
have you seen her eyes?
she holds wisdom in her irises, and one look tells you her whole lifetime.
do you know what she has fought for?
she has fought for freedom. she has fought for peace.
she escaped through her childhood bedroom window and never turned back.
she has found her state of mind, sitting in her own red rose garden.
she rocks her **red velvet** lip gloss, remembering the strength she needed to get here.

-02/27/2023

my room has grown smaller.

here i am again, sitting in my dark, dry room.
the walls have closed in, and the space has grown more dreadful.
i still stare at the ceiling, waiting for the day i can escape.
i don't feel real anymore, and the overwhelming fear of
failure keeps me glued to my bed.
i need to get out, and finally have some peace. i can't do
this anymore.
my throat is too dry, my lips are too chapped.
my headache is growing more powerful, and my stomach
groans with hunger.
i can't remember the last time i did my makeup or wore a
pair of jeans.
maybe when i escape from dunnburr street, i can finally
be happy.

-02/27/2023

graduate;

i never thought this day would come,
dressed in blue.
i toss my cap as a salute of success.

i did it everyone. i did it.

back when it felt like i couldn't breathe,
and when sadness and confusion was the only emotion in
my heart,
i thought i would fail.

but i didn't.

i will walk, i will smile, and i will succeed.
i will make a future for myself.
i will do it as payment for my past self,
for losing her hope, her innocence, and her happiness.

congratulations to i, for staying strong and not taking myself
out of this world.

i will grow, and i will not perish.

-05/26/2023

the first snow

i am like the first snowfall in november.
my heart is chilled and heavy; six inches fallen onto my chest.
frostbitten, broken am i,
pondering why the powder is so cold.
i ache immensely, as the negative temperatures are too harsh
on sensitive nature.
dormant and secluded, the visibility covered in white dust.
i am the first snowfall.

-08/22/2023

domified my identity

the smell of home is starting to rub off my sweaters.
the nights grew quieter.
the days grew lonelier.
you are a big girl now,
you do not need a shoulder to cry on.
you are independent now,
you are doing this for your future.

what if i want a hand to hold?
am i supposed to wipe my tears and keep going without
any composure?

i guess i will,
as i have nobody here but me,
miles away from the place i call home.

-08/29/2023

deadbeat: change deadbolt

i sulk into my new identity.
a new version of myself that still doesn't include you.
you haven't been here for any new fazes of my sentience.

i still ponder if you are using opiates, or if you have
recovered but still hesitate to come back.
even if you did return…

the deadbolt lock would never be opened.

we have changed the locks to every door and secured
every window.
you cannot leave for nine years and then bounce back like it
has been nine minutes.

it doesn't matter how much the clock has ticked, or how
many times the sun has orbited earth.
we will never forget.
the trauma and fear will always leave a residue on our home.

-08/29/2023

cinderella story

she ran away from infidelity.
she skipped down the ballroom stairs leaving everything behind.
she dropped her glass slipper, but she was too scattered to
care, maybe even to notice.
it poured rain the night of her disappearance.
nobody knew she was gone; the only evidence was her
glass slipper.
the man she left saw the slipper, and knew it was hers.
he didn't want her to be found, so he crushed the glass with
his steel boots.
she was never found, living in despair alone in the dark,
cold forest.

-09/23/2023

forever scraped and scathed.

letting go is the best choice i've made but worry still scrapes at my skin.
the thought of leaving being a wrong move gouache into me, making my heart bleed.

i mourn the loss of your love.

even though our love cut my soul into a million pieces, i still enjoyed the experience.

i wonder if life will ever be the same, now that i'm scarred and damaged goods.

will anybody appreciate me although i have slices in my skin?

my tears are starting to form scabs, healing from your sharpness.

will my wounds leave a nasty scar, or will i someday be completely whole again?

-09/26/2023

yin

(year of 2033)
my hair flows in the wind on an autumn evening,
and i investigate the horizon.
my soft skin feels the breeze, a perfect day equipped
with a crisp warmth.
i see ombré in the sunset, and **i smile at the sky.**
standing next to me is not you, but someone else.
he is kind. he is loving. **his smile lights up my entire life.**
he holds my hand as we watch the world, standing on the
porch of our dream home we built together.

i made an **amazing** choice that day back in september of
twenty-twenty-three.
i left you, so i had the opportunity to meet him.
i took the chance of never finding love again.
i made a leap into the abyss, and i made it.
i am happy.

but what if…this isn't the outcome.
but what if…my life was **yang instead of yin?**

-09/26/2023

yang

(year of 2033)
my cheek is seared with a harsh burn.
the burn is of a man's hand striking my cheek.
i wince in pain and hold my face with **immense regret.**
a tear streams down, and i wipe it quickly before he notices.
i am screamed at for my every move. **i am in danger daily.**
i feel so **anguished, abused, and terrified.**
my heart sinks into oblivion, my understanding being that
this will be my life forever.

it is all because of the decision i made in september of
twenty-twenty-three.
i left you, so i had the destiny to meet him.
i took the chance of never finding love again.
i made a leap into the abyss, and i fell into a trap.
i fell into domestic violence, poverty, and depression.

but what if…this isn't the outcome.
but what if…my life was **yin instead of yang?**

-09/26/2023

i'm sorry darlin

darlin, i'm not sure what to do.
infidelity lurks in my head.
i feel my passion for you diminishing day to day.
i eye others and imagine what it would be like with them in
place of you.
darlin, i don't think i love you anymore.
if i truly loved you, i wouldn't want another man.
i'm sorry darlin, but i must break your heart.
i don't want to be a deceiver, a cheater.
darlin, i must sacrifice you for your own sake.
i don't want to break you into pieces.
i instead break you in half,
so you can put yourself back together over time.
i'm sorry darlin.
goodbye.

hello lust.
i haven't seen you in a while.
it's time to talk again,
i've been missing you.

-09/27/2023

without you

happiness is without you.
without you is bliss.
i can feel the breeze without shivers running down my spine.
i can touch the world with my fingers without remorse.
you cannot repo my joy anymore.
i took control of my sails.
i am in control.
and i love it.
freedom is without you.
without you is peace.

-10/16/2023

was it worth it?

everything is new.
i feel like i have been reborn.
i haven't breathed fresh air since i was fifteen.
i now am a technical adult, pondering my experience at eighteen.
was it worth it to love you?
was it worth it to lose everyone for your attention?
was it worth it to listen to your demands,
to gain your approval?
was it worth losing myself for you?

i feel so lost.
i'm the happiest i've ever been,
but i can't help but feel lonely.
life without you is easy,
but it feels like solitude.

-10/17/2023

secret back at home

i'd love to be your other girl,
but i've got somewhere to go.
i'd love to fuel your **sick fantasy of infidelity,**
but i have plans those days.

i wish you would've kept your relationship a secret, so my
innocent lust wasn't shattered into pieces.
i thought we were getting to know each other.
i thought we could have become something more.
you mislead my heart, like many others before.

it turns out you have a lover back at home.
i am your college distraction.
you are not interested in my heart.
you just want **something to entertain you** while your real
girl is away.

i wish i didn't feel guilty for something **i didn't know.**
my passion would have **never touched you** if i knew she
existed.
the poor girl...
her "soulmate" is **playing the field** without her knowledge.

i am sorry i like you.
i am sorry i wanted more with you.
i am not apologizing to you though,
i am apologizing to your other half.

-10/24/2023

114

the jungle

every time i find someone i think is genuine,
it all gets revealed in a twisted vine-like manner.
i don't think love is real.
if it is, i don't think there is any one for me.
i search and pounce on every opportunity i get.
they ruin it swiftly.
my heart gets ripped to shreds,
and i am left a touch more hopeless.

-10/24/2023

you're too sweet to turn sour...

we had everything in common.
our pasts intertwined even though they were never connected.
we could be serious, talking about our trauma and heartache.
we could be playful, teasing each other on who is better.
we could be anything.
but…it was too good to be true.

i was getting led on and lied to.
i can't call you out on the mishap,
because no official lie was ever spoken.

you withheld the truth from my ears.
you warped my perception of reality.
you technically didn't commit the crime.
you didn't perform the incriminating actions.

i know your intentions though.
although it wasn't an official lie,
i was still manipulated and teased endlessly.

-10/24/2023

rehab

recover, recover, recover.
words that have been spewed at me for nearly a decade.

i enjoy dancing in the kitchen at 4 a.m. with my blood
pumping; my heart racing a marathon.

the opiates i inject into my forearms make me forget; i do not
want to remember the pain i have inflicted on others.

i have gone to rehab before…i have tried the recovery lifestyle.
they will never trust me again. honestly i don't even trust myself.

people who become sober are never completely forgiven;
why give up the euphoria for a harsh reality?

i would rather die alone and high. i am sick of the ever
long suffering.
i am a reject to society. i will never live up to the expectations
everyone had of me.

-11/07/2023

darkness is a cold blanket

i am the dull cloud that foreshadows the sun.
i am the dread you feel before a daunting task.

i have been turned black and white.
evil people have drained the color out of me.

i was once sunshine; i am now a thunderstorm.

time and time again i gave away my colors.
red, orange, yellow, green, blue...

i am a sponge that has been squeezed and dried.

i hope to find a palette to fulfill me again.
the love and passion exist somewhere in this world.

i hope i can be brought to life with vivid imagery.

-11/07/2023

constant terror

i still have nightmares about you every night.
i escaped you in reality; you still haunt my consciousness.

no matter how many pictures i erase; no matter how many
sentimental items are discarded.

you terrorize me nightly.

will i ever be released from your grasp?

even with zero contact, no way to communicate.

you have a hold on me that is sickening.

-11/08/2023

my heart pits itself against me

i wonder why i make these decisions.
i put myself in impossible places.
i have to wiggle myself out of the terror.

i fell for a boy; he doesn't even know.
i cannot have him, and i knew that from the get-go.

he doesn't think of me; he doesn't care for me.
although, he haunts my dreams every night.
he lives in my mind like a record; he sits in my consciousness
twenty-four-seven.
it doesn't matter if i'm awake or asleep.

i imagine a future with you.
but you have one planned with someone else.

why do i end up in these scenarios?
why can't i fall for something i can actually have?

-11/13/2023

something about you

there is something about you.
ever since the first day i lied eyes on you
i was drawn to you.

i feel that there is nothing that could make me stop
pondering your existence.
i feel like you are my destiny.

i know it sounds like bullshit.
i know it sounds like i am a lunatic.
but i feel something there; something different than i have
ever felt before.

it's a longing; there is determination to have you all to myself.
i am confident i will get you.
even though it is very unlikely.

-11/14/2023

why miss the one who cut me?

it's weird to think about you since you've been gone.
you were by my side day and night.
you moved in almost immediately; we shared our bed for
years.
imagining your freckles, your eyes, your hands, your skin on
mine.
it hurts. i will never touch you again.

it was my choice, the breakup.
i am the one who pulled the trigger.
i know it was a right shot.

i wasn't prepared to see the wounds; to see you bleeding out
pleading for me to stay.

you had a grip on me; a control stronger than anything.
i somehow escaped your wrath.
but i still miss you.
maybe it's your manipulation talking in my head.
because i know damn well i am better off without you.

-11/15/2023

'him' is not you.

i miss you—well, not you.
i miss him.
'him' was the thought of you in my head.
'him' was a man that wanted to marry me.
he was willing to do anything for my love.

you are not the same as him.
you are a narcissist, a liar, a deceiver.
you twisted my words into something you wanted to hear.

he may have been an aspect of you;
though not the truthful man.

the truth of you is something more sinister;
you are something that makes me quiver.

you live a persona i couldn't even imagine partaking in.

i miss him—though 'him' wasn't ever there.
it was just you.

-11/18/2023

no gratification will come.

why can't i just get what i want for once?
i wish and pray for better days.
they never come.

everything i want is never handed to me.
i always i think i almost have it; right when i almost reach
gratification, **it is ripped away.**

even if i work for what i want,
it somehow doesn't happen the way it should.

my heart is getting sick and tired of this endless bullshit.

i cry and cry **hoping that god will feel the ache** i have in
my chest.

please just end this suffering i feel every day.
the weight of my trauma sinks into my soul.

-11/18/2023

about the author

Faith Foley started writing poetry with a writing assignment in eighth grade; her first poetry collection, *reflections*, was published by Legacy Book Press LLC in 2020. She is currently attending St. Ambrose University in Davenport, Iowa, on a full tuition scholarship, studying early childhood education where she also participates in dance marathon and works with kindergartners as a student teacher. When she's not studying, teaching, writing poetry, or raising money for the University of Iowa Hospital's young patients, she enjoys expressing her creativity through painting and drawing as well as spending time with her three chickens, Miko, Jupiter, and Whopper. In addition to her dorm room, Faith lives with her dad; dog, Hope; and sister, Isabel, in Iowa. Her other sisters, Maddie and Justine, also live in Iowa.